THE REVIVAL OF THE PROPHET TO THE NATIONS

Series Introduction

Many of us have been trained so well in the prophetic that even God's silence speaks to us. We've learned to find God in the rhythm and the cadence of the quiet. We're unmoved, unshaken, and undisturbed because we can discern the Word of the Lord even in a dark place.

The level of revelation that Jesus has given us in the modern restoration of the prophetic ministry is unparalleled. Revelatory impartation has given the body of Christ new realms of sensitivity that prior generations longed for.

We are living in what those who are asleep prayed for. We may not be where we want to, but God certainly has taken us somewhere. Many premier prophetic voices have led movements training us to discern the activity of the Spirit and gauge what God is saying and what he's doing.

The prophetic saves lives. God used it to save mine and if you're reading this book, he probably used it to save yours at some point, too. In fact, prophets and prophetic people have been traveling across the country and the world to declare the Word of the Lord with accuracy and power. Countless lives have been saved and deliverance has taken the people of God to new dimensions and realms.

God's prophets preach with boldness, declare with fire and rescue many from the violent flames of hell into the arms of our loving Father. I look forward to seeing the continued progression and growth of prophets and the prophetic movement. It seems that as a body we've attained a high level of mastery in personal prophecy.

However, the acumen of many prophetic voices to speak into the lives and destinies of so many with accuracy and clarity has given us a hubris that impedes our ability to restore a significant role of integrity to the office of the prophet. It's time to see the revival of the prophet to the nations. Not merely prophets that prophesy to the body Christ in churches, but prophets like Daniel and Isaish who release the word of the Lord to the kings and the princes of the Earth.

The COVID-19 pandemic has exposed grave immaturity in America's prophetic movement. Many of God's prophets are too politically biased to be trusted to minister on a regional, national, or international scale regarding governments and institutions outside of the church walls. Many of the prophets who speak on such matters have profound ministries of personal prophecy that save lives but lack the jurisdiction to move in the governmental counsel. Unfortunately, some of these prophets who have been called to particular nations have become so biased by their political, socio-economic, and even doctrinal views that they would never be trusted by a genuine leader in a crisis. The prophet has always had a responsibility to the believer, but I believe we've neglected their responsibility to the unbeliever, particularly with regard to cities, governments, and nations. It's time for the prophets to the nations to arise again. In the days old, prophets were so accurate that they were literally respected by the heads of state to give counsel. God wants to restore the office of the prophet to the nations, but we must first go through a cleansing. This series of books is written to help those who are prophetic in nature to be free from their own personal and political biases that hinder their ability to go beyond the political climate and what they see with their eyes.

Book 1: COVID-19, End Times Hysteria, and the Christian Church: How Conspiracy Theories are Destroying the Credibility of the Prophetic Movement

In this book, I use the COVID-19 epidemic as a case

study to explain how attaching conspiracy theories to the Word of the Lord is a dangerous and unacceptable practice for the prophetic movement. I explain the state of global affairs in both an academic and spiritual context as I analyze what I believe to be errors in the prophetic movement.

Book 2: The Politicization of the American Prophetic Movement

In the second book of this series, I discuss the concerning trend of the prophetic movement that has married God's holy office with partisan politics. I explain how prophetic directions and instruction should never be biased or tainted by personal or corporate political views.

Book 3: Unmasking Prophetic Bias

In the third book, I go into further detail on the keys to managing the biases that we all have and keeping them away from the flow of prophecy. Personal opinion should never be confused with or pronounced as a prophecy. Many prophetic ministers miss the mark here and fall into error.

Book 4: How to be a Prophet to the Nations: A Guidebook for Ministering to Executives and World Leaders

A prophet called to minister in the government sector must be groomed in a unique way. God deals with them differently and speaks to them differently. This class of prophet must carry themselves differ-

COVID-19, End Times Hysteria, and the Christian Church:

How Conspiracy Theories Are Destroying the Credibility of the Prophetic Movement

First Printing, 2020

ISBN 978-0-578-72198-9

ently to handle their weight of responsibility. Chief of which, this class of prophet must be able to speak the language of government or else they will never be called on by any reputable sources outside of the church.

THERE'S BLOOD ON OUR HANDS

There's blood on the hands of preachers all across America. How can we be watchmen for the people of God if we say peace and safety when there should be an alarm going off? If the nation's watchmen declare peace when people should run, they're playing for the wrong team. I believe that due to arrogance, misinformation, and a lust for end-times calamity, many leaders in high places have been steering the flock of God in the wrong direction.There are many leaders, even prophetic ones, who have not discerned the gravity of the crisis the world is facing. Misinformation is clouding the perception and sensitivity of key leaders in the American church.

As an international relations prophet, hearing God regarding governments and policy is a regular occurrence in my daily life. It's a primary discussion that I have with the Lord. I wake up to visions of political events that I see on the news shortly after I begin my day. The Lord shows me specific events in the future, difficulties that key leaders face, and solutions to problems that are to come. International relations prophecy is not something that I visit every once and a while. It's a place that I live in.

Before you rush to call me arrogant, I'm speaking not to make myself out to be some so-called "master" prophet that everyone should listen to, but rather to help you understand my perspective better.

My concern is that many prophets and prophetic people who are not mantled to handle public policy issues are speaking out in a lane that God did not call them to. Because they're in the wrong jurisdiction, they're speaking in error. While many have mastered personal prophecy, certainly far better than I, their ability to accurately declare the word of the Lord concerning global policy issues seems to be immature.

I respectfully agree to disagree with most popular prophecies circulating regarding COVID-19's origin because most of the prophetic voices speaking are far too familiar with baseless conspiracy theory websites. In short, I believe that most of them have attached the phrase, "*the Lord said*" to something the Lord isn't actually saying. Instead, it's something their soul agreed with on a conspiracy theory website.

I also believe that many around these prophetic voices heard what one or a few have said from these websites and have regurgitated those words as if God spoke it directly to them.

I don't expect everyone to agree with me because many who've released soulish words regarding the coronavirus pandemic have a greater tenure in their prophetic career than I.

My aim is not necessarily to make you agree with me and disagree with them, but more so to encourage you to become more prudent every time you open your mouth to say "thus saith the Lord" or even share a post on social media. I don't believe prophetic people understand the weight of responsibility that they carry when they prophesy.

Although you may have preconceived notions regarding the prophetic and COVID-19, this book should be read with humility and sobriety to gain anything from it. If we're going to be reliable prophetic vessels, we can't only consume ourselves in concepts that we prefer to listen to or else we'll be bound by our personal opinions and not open to new ones, even opinions that come from God. Therefore, if my views or explanations bother you, that means you should probably keep reading.

As you will see me explain later, even if some of the prophecies that people have released somehow turn out to be correct, we still have significant concerns to discuss regarding the source and authenticity of much of what has been said. It's one thing to get a prophetic word from God and release that to the people. It's another thing to read conspiracy theory websites, quicken a little bit, and regurgitate concepts from those blogs as if they're prophecies.

In this book, I discuss the troubling relationship between the prophetic movement and misinformation. Furthermore I explain that not only do we refuse to properly judge prophecy, we also refuse to fact check information that appeals to our biases. I also discuss the spiritual ramifications of downplaying the impact of the pandemic. In section two, I discuss the danger of misinformation and compare fact from fiction from an academic perspective. In the last section, I leave you with parting wisdom for pastors and leaders as they navigate the crisis and a closing prophetic word.

THE PANDEMIC OF MISINFORMATION

It would be almost impossible to discuss and research every single COVID-19 conspiracy theory and piece of misinformation that exists. Everyone has created their own perspective and view of what, when, where, and why regardless of the facts at hand. In the United States, many believe the virus is a deep state creation to hurt President Trump's re-election campaign. However, there are others that swear that the virus was bioengineered in a lab in Wuhan, China. Let's not forget the idea that COVID-19 was somehow caused by 5G. Oddly enough I know people that believe in all of the above even though they can't all be true at the same time.

Of course, coronavirus theories aren't limited to the United States. Some Iranian thought leaders accused the United States of bioengineering the virus to inflict harm on their country. There are also those that believe the United States created the virus in order to cripple China's reputation and economy in a new escalation to the on-going trade war. Regardless of what country, demographic, or ethnic group you speak to, everyone has a perspective on the origins of this new invisible enemy. The perspective is typical of where they live in the world, the geopolitical interests of the country they live in or abiding distrust they have for their government or globalism.

The body of Christ is no different. We're in this world, not of it, but still, we represent a microcosm of the global population. If you take just a few minutes to browse evangelical Twitter or Facebook, you'll be inundated with blogs and articles on the latest coronavirus conspiracy theories. You'll see a plethora of YouTube videos by doctors with highly questionable medical credentials, but strong political ties, provide the "real" information about what's going on. They're here to make sure that the people of God know what's really going on.

I'm not surprised that doctors who practice internal medicine only, and have no background in epidemiology nor any published scientific research papers, seem to be so eager to be dissenting voices in the eyes of the political base they serve. The reality is that a brief background check on their scientific pedigree, medical history, and analysis of their publications often exposes their limited knowledge on the subject matter and credibility concerns.

I know what you're going to say next, "Of course! The

deep state blacklisted them and planted that trail just so we wouldn't trust them!" That's the funny thing about conspiracy theories. Once you're biased to believing them you look for information that proves what you're predetermined notions are. So, even evidence that that disproves the credibility of something that you believe in now becomes fuel to further believe the conspiracy theory.

Here we begin trying to pull you out of the rabbit trail of delusion and obsession because you refuse to accept any information that runs contrary to what you already believe. Our culture has developed a lust to be "woke," which means to have knowledge or information that only a few people have. This desire to be an enlightened one who is set apart from the masses causes people to receive information blindly.

"Now the serpent was more crafty than any other beast of the field that the Lord God had made. He said to the woman, "Did God actually say, 'You shall not eat of any tree in the garden'?" 2 And the woman said to the serpent, "We may eat of the fruit of the trees in the garden, 3 but God said, 'You shall not eat of the fruit of the tree that is in the midst of the garden, neither shall you touch it, lest you die.'" 4 But the serpent said to the woman, "You will not surely die. 5 For God knows that when you eat of it your eyes will be opened, and you will be like God, knowing good and evil."
-Genesis 3:1-5

Do you understand that the first conspiracy theory began in the garden? Satan had some secret information that he wanted to give to Eve. You see the mainstream thought was that Elohim was the Author, Creator, and Father with the best interest in mind. Satan came with a new thought to challenge the old narrative and enlighten the human race with a false reality.

Satan is the author of suspicion and mistrust of information that God wants us to rely on. He wants us to question God and His motives. Once we open up to his alternative reality, we will call real news fake and fake news real. The serpent intends to get America to fall for a demonic distrust of anything or anyone that speaks with authority.

The problem is that once you accept his narrative, then you'll be bound by whatever deceptive forces he employs to govern his storyline- whether pride, perversion, or fear. The reason I'm writing this book is because the Father shared with me in prayer that the people of God are easily attracted to conspiracy theories because they gain a feeling of superiority for having supposed secret knowledge.

Satan promised Eve that she would be like God and have hidden information that would make her special. Like Eve, many in the prophetic movement have taken the bait and relied on invalid information straight from the kingdom of hell because it has massaged their egos.

Satan has and always will use the false light of misinformation to recruit new teammates even if the teammates don't recognize who they're playing for.

And no wonder, for even Satan disguises
himself as an angel of light.
- 2 Corinthians 14:11

The devil is well skilled at making himself and other forms of darkness appear to emit light. He loves to give information that sounds deep and revelatory, but when fact-checked it's biased, false, delusional, and dangerous. He promised Eve enlightenment but gave her darkness.

We are in an American culture and a church climate that gains a feeling of superiority to other people who are less "enlightened" because they aren't "woke." In reality, in an attempt to be contrarian and countercultural, many rely on blogs and media outlets that are politically or theologically biased in a way that doesn't give them the intellectual curiosity to properly fact check their information or question their own views. People rely on information that panders toward their biases and their carnality.

In a severely partisan time in our nation's history, the masters of alternative media are skilled at making money on Christians looking to have their opinions reinforced and their delusions affirmed.

We've come to a place where research based peer-reviewed studies are considered to be no more than fake news. Reporting based on valid sources and credible research is deemed to be invalid because it doesn't meet the narrative of a deep state end times conspiracy that the church thrives on.

We're in a time where people are desperately desiring to confirm the views that they already harbor. They're one google search and Facebook algorithm away from being presented with the ideas and concepts they wish to believe which are reinforced through a digital culture that has no discernment.

Conspiracy theories have far reaching mental ramifications that have the propensity to add an erroneous bias to the sensitivity and discernment of prophets and prophetic people. It is our prophetic responsibility to keep our spiritual gifts, communication with God, and access to the supernatural realm bias free or we will endanger the lives of others.

Conspiracy theorists take advantage of a psychological concept known as the illusory truth effect. That is the more a false statement is repeated, the more we start to believe that statement is true.[1] A significant factor in how we judge whether a statement is valid is based on how many times we've heard the statement.[2]

In other words, if we repeatedly listen to false information we will be more likely to believe that information is valid regardless of how baseless the claim is. Research shows that this tendency is coded into the human brain to help us process information better. However, it can also lead to very smart people believing dumb things. Further studies on the illusory truth effect suggest that "knowledge does not protect against illusory truth."[3]

That means that our intelligence and analytic ability has a tendency to bow down to things that we've heard multiple times, whether they're true or not, even if we know better. Spirit-filled, tongue speaking believers are not immune to the psychology of the human brain.

This humbling fact should make those of us with the responsibility to release the Word of the Lord on public platforms very cautious about the information that we allow ourselves to be exposed to. Prophetic people should avoid consuming information from conspiracy theory websites because they are recalibrating what we believe to be true.

If exposure can damage your natural discernment, why risk these websites from making an impact on your spiritual senses? The carnal desire to have the supposed secret truths is hurting the accuracy and global reputation of the prophetic movement.

Just like our poor habit of not judging prophecy, we don't judge any of the information that we read or watch, especially if it's coming from an alternative source. We have a tendency to discredit mainstream information without any credible empirical, statistical, and scientific evidence, but accept unresearched opinions and hysteria from credential-less authors without thinking twice.

Take for instance one of the most popular conspiracy theory websites, InfoWars. During the COVID-19 pandemic, so many articles from websites like this were readily shared by prophetic people. A further examination of InfoWars and similar sites should show us that we ought not rely on them for news.

After the 2012 Sandy Hook shooting, which killed 20 children between the ages of 6-7 and six adults, InfoWars intently peddled a conspiracy theory that the shooting was a hoax. Without remorse, the founder Alex Jones claimed that "no one died" and that the victims were "child actors."[4][5] Jones's incendiary remarks which reached his millions of followers led to the harassment of many of the parents who lost their children in the shooting. One of the parents, Jeremy Richman, even committed suicide.

In court documents from suits against Alex Jones, the founder revealed some of the sources by which he bases his research. His investigations appear to go no further than speaking with other conspiracy theorists, people who email him, and anonymous messengers on internet forums like 4chan.[6] In other words, Alex relies on paranoid people who are full of suspicion and bias to report false claims that millions now look to for news.

He used information from random people in a way that tormented families who were already grieving. Alex has since walked back his claims acknowledging "children died and it's a tragedy."[7] He blames psychosis for his conspiratorial obsessions. In his deposition for lawsuits by Sandyhook parents he says "And I, myself, have almost had like a form of psychosis back in the past where I basically thought everything was staged, even though I've now learned a lot of times things aren't staged."[8] Despite the pain his misinformation website has caused, InfoWars still has not taken down its false Sandy Hook articles as a reputable traditional news outlet would do.

This is because InfoWars is not a news website. As Mr. Jones mentioned in his deposition he is a "pundit" and his "opinions have been wrong." Alex Jones and other conspiracy theorists are not intending to state the truth, but rather use their platform to share their soulish opinions.

InfoWars and other conspiracy theory websites, unfortunately have a hand in corrupting the prophetic movement. It seems as if in many instances people are led more by Alex Jones than by the Holy Spirit. I've seen many seasoned prophetic voices begin to share "news" stories and articles from InfoWars and similar sites. Subsequently, they begin to prophecy according to the information that they're reading. The same website that promoted the idea that a mass shooting where several children were murdered was a hoax is the same website claiming that Bill Gates is somehow behind the novel coronavirus.

Similar websites use the same type of baseless "research" to promote the concept that COVID-19 is some grand government conspiracy. The pattern that I see is this: prophetic people read these articles, get stirred in their flesh, and regurgitate the information by saying, "The Lord said 'COVID-19 is a hoax to get us to accept the mark of the beast!'" This is nothing new however. Conspiracy theories have been fueling the prophetic movement for a while (more on that in book two). Some of the older prophetic voices claimed that social security number was the mark of the beast. That word didn't stand the test of time just like many of the words being released now won't either.

Prophetic voices have partnered with a destructive spirit of confusion and misinformation to release words that have the potential to kill people. The issue is that we don't just want a word from a spirit, or a word from someone's soul, we need a word from the Lord.

Prophets have the responsibility of walking in integrity with the Word of the Lord or they will transfer mantles of error in the dark days to come. In the future, when the world is most in need of the prophetic, the sons of the preceding generations will be viewed as the sheep who cried wolf because of the delusion of their prophetic fathers.

If our prophets rely on misinformation to prophecy, their warnings will eventually fall on deaf ears, exposing the generation to come to death, destruction, and chaos. If God's prophets fall to delusion, what hope does the rest of the body have?

WHERE ARE
THE JUDGES?

There are many bizarre origin stories of COVID-19 being championed among both conspiracy theorists and prophetic voices. When I scroll on my timeline, I see countless leaders sharing videos from conspiracy theorists and many going as far as to specifically say things like, "The Lord said Bill Gates created the coronavirus because he's an evil man looking to control the population."

One of the reasons I believe the credibility of the prophetic movement is in danger is because so few people are saying the same thing. Maybe your timeline is in unison, but even as I look at the words released by well-known prophetic voices, the only thing that unites them is that they sound just like conspiracy theory websites, albeit with different commentary.

Some prophets say Gates and Fauchi are behind the disease. Others say they saw the disease bioengineered in a lab. Even among those who sound as if they received the same revelation express totally different motives. For instance, several prophets have said the virus was bioengineered in a lab. Of those some say the Lord told them that the virus escaped by accident. Others believe the Lord told them that the virus was intentionally released by the Chinese for economic motives. Ironically, some of these prophets at the same time prophesy that Gates and Fauchi are behind the virus which is a total contraction. If these were the days of the Old Testament, when prophecy was still taken seriously, and all their COVID-19 prophetic words were written on one scroll, there would be obvious contradictions.

One such prophet who claimed to have seen a conspiracy even went as far to say that the virus would leave by March 27th. As the pandemic continued beyond that date, the prophet then adjusted his statement, claiming that he actually meant that the virus would only leave Wuhan by that date. At the time of this writing, China is actually enacting extreme mitigation measures because of a new cluster of cases in Wuhan.[9] Doctors in north China are also dealing with a potential mutation of the virus with a longer incubation period. Many of the prophetic words regarding COVID-19 simply just don't add up.

I'm not saying that these leaders aren't prophets (for the most part, some actually are not). I'm not saying that they don't hear from God. I'm not saying that God doesn't use them in tremendous ways. I am saying I believe that we as the body are missing the mark by speaking outside of our realm of spiritual jurisdiction. We're speaking on matters that we don't thoroughly understand and we're confusing the spirit of suspicion with the discernment of spirits.

I've found very few prophetic voices who spoke of a pandemic scale virus occurring before the outbreak began in December 2019. The majority of prophecies that I've found began in or around February 2020. The prophets that I know of who specifically foresaw a viral pandemic, before December 2019 made no mention of the origins of the virus, neither did they mention any conspiracy theories. They simply prophesied concerning the virus and key impacts on society.

With that being said, I'm relatively skeptical of most of the current prophetic words released. The sad part is this: if there are prophetic voices that have genuinely discerned foul play regarding the current global crisis that have not bowed to the spirit of suspicion nor to the political views of the culture, they're being drowned out by the many voices that should be in silence right now.

They could be drowned out by prophetic voices that are more in-tune to the views of their favorite political party than the voice of the Lord. They could be drowned out by the many prophetic voices relying on misinformation for the source of the spiritual insight. Or they might be drowned out by prophetic voices who feel the pressure to say something even if God hasn't spoken to them.

Over the course of COVID-19, I've literally seen prophetic voices, whom I once thought were credible, post information from conspiracy theory websites as prophetic words from the Lord. They took global gossip which made an agreement with the carnal place within them and called misinformation the Word the Lord. We shouldn't be copying and pasting articles as prophetic words or adding a prophetic declaration to a post that's based on misinformation. These tactics cripple the credibility of true words from God.

It is the pride of having to be "the prophet" that causes many to subtly fall into error.They feel they must speak and are willing to conjure up something in the soul to satisfy the demand from people. Unfortunately, they are only fueled by personal ego.

If some of these words based on misguided information turn out to be true, we must understand that it's not because God honors them as prophetic words. In actuality, they are hearsay based on misinformation, not prophecy. We ought to be concerned that these prophetic voices may be encouraged to continue to gaze into the crystal ball of conspiracy theory websites to inform their prophetic lusts.

The prophetic movement has conflicting views on America's political climate, the current COVID-19 crisis, and the response of the church because not everyone is pulling from the same source. The agenda of the one who prophesies determines the source they choose to prophesy from, whether earthly, carnal, and fleshly, or from the spirit of the living God. The Spirit of God transcends not just time and space, but human bias and limitation. He should be the source of light and revelation for the prophet.

Critical prophetic voices of our time have brought the body of Christ comfort, exhortation, and clarity in the midst of critical storms. Through prophetic words, lives have been inexplicably changed. Being a mouthpiece for God is a responsibility that we ought never take lightly. Once we belittle the weight of what God has called us to do, we're prone to make space for pride and fall into error.

Accuracy is a prophetic responsibility. There is a remnant of people eager to live their lives in accordance to everything that God says. They shape and conform their lives to His instruction. They quake and tremble at His voice and only want to do His will. Whether perfect or imperfect, in joy or grief, they make a way to press into the ordinances of the Most High. We often talk about how casual, jaded, and callous our Christianity is (and it definitely is those things), but we need to recognize the fact that there are people recklessly pursuing God.

They left the comfort of their careers, families, and personal definitions of success to follow a loving, but invisible God who often speaks in mysteries and parables. They've given up everything to pursue Jesus regardless of what's going on in and around them. They have everything to lose and they're ready to obey. Regardless of the disheartening church attendance statistics and array of both public and private leadership failures occurring in the American church, there are people crying out to God with a profound hunger and thirst for righteousness. They have a Holy Spirit inspired zeal that causes them to run through troops like David and leap over walls. It's not right to harm them with false prophecies that stem from pride or imagination.

God has lavishly poured out His spirit upon this generation. The Lord has shown me much more revival to come, but for a moment let us consider where we've come from since the dark ages where revelation was shut up. God restored the function of the church and the role of the pastor. The Lord raised up generals like Tyndale, who literally gave up their lives, so that the Bible could be read by the common man. We've seen revivals of healing and miracles. There's even been a revival of the office of the teacher. Most recently, we've also seen the restoration of both the apostolic and prophetic offices.

Although this is not a comprehensive summary of revival or church history, we can say that as time has passed, God has graced us with great power and He's meeting the hunger demand that the chosen ones of this generation are crying out for. It is for those who are hungry that I am writing this series of books for. They are hungry and their great zeal isn't always "according to knowledge" as the Apostle Paul spoke of the people of his day.

We have to protect the zealous among us who are growing in knowledge and ready to obey the word of the Lord prophetically. Therefore, leaders have the prophetic responsibility to be accurate when they speak. There must be a culture of prophetic integrity where leaders are honest and direct when they are certain, but forthcoming and cautious when they are unsure what God is saying. We have the responsibility to stay within the confines of our office and not try to be an expert in matters that we are not fully acquainted with because of our prophetic roles.

Brain surgeons are brilliant people in my estimation, but I don't want them fixing my car because although their training was rigorous and demanding, their rank and expertise in medicine holds no weight when it comes to the world of mechanics.

Many of today's leaders are speaking far outside of

their prophetic jurisdiction and it's causing confusion and chaos. People live and die by what men and women of God say because of the position that we hold in their lives. Because people esteem the Word of God and our role as "stewards of the mysteries of God," we must come to understand that we can be graced by God to steward the revelation of God's Word, but not be graced as professionals to counsel people on everything. Most ministry leaders are not mental health professionals, doctors, or policy experts, but many speak authoritatively in these areas as if they're spiritual credentials transfer over into every arena of life.

I believe a major problem in today's prophetic movement is that there are many apostolic and prophetic leaders who are speaking in the wrong jurisdiction. They are commenting on matters they don't even have a surface level of understanding on and they have the saints of God walking in unnecessary suspicion of the government, the media, and even medicine. The problem is that suspicion is neither a fruit nor a gift of the Holy Spirit.

We must be very careful to understand the weight that our words and counsel can have because even our advice at times can be innocently taken as the Word of the Lord to those who follow us. Your suspicion can become their carnality. Your distrust can become their anger. What may be managed in you can be out of control in the people who are looking to hear God through you.

There is a grave danger in peering outside of the office that God has given us and assuming the status of expert in something that we know little about. We live in a culture where we've been deceived by the power of a google search. Just because we can search for information, read a few articles and watch a few videos doesn't mean we thoroughly understand a topic enough to give counsel on it or even form an opinion about it in some cases.

The pressures and responsibilities that come with crisis often reveal old problems and unresolved issues that existed before the situation began. The COVID-19 pandemic has revealed significant defects in the prophetic movement that need to be promptly addressed or the American church will be in danger of passing on watered down, feasible, inconsistent, and politically biased prophetic mantles that will be unreliable for the crises of the coming days.

While we have done a fair amount of training on prophetic ministry, a major problem seems to be that too few prophetic people are capable of judging prophecy. If you look at the many erroneous and soulish prophetic words motivated by fear, greed, selfish ambition, paranoia, and political bias on social media, you can see that even seasoned prophetic voices have a tendency to partner with prophetic words that they have not first judged.

As men and women of God around the globe continue to prophecy and train in the prophetic ministry, there must be a greater emphasis on teaching the people of God how to judge and detect the nature of the flesh and soul that has crept into many prophetic circles. Our metric for judging prophecy cannot be a prophetic person's platform alone.

There are many so-called prophets with large platforms that are very weak in the prophetic. I remember being completely shocked at a service I attended because one such minister had a Word of knowledge that seemed to be accurate only 50% of the time and the majority of the prophecies he released had at least one error in them. My prophetic colleagues looked at me in bewilderment as we discerned the same thing.

Despite the very obvious errors that he made, people received what he said because he had a major name, platform, and the word lined up with their desires. It is not sustainable to continue to have so many activations and training on the gifts of the spirit and the supernatural without having the prophets, prophetic people, and the body of Christ at large be a better toolkit to judge prophetic words.

Another issue in prophetic culture is that prophets who minister especially regarding current events, policy matters, and issues of a political nature tend to use words that they've heard from other people, without judging them, as if God spoke that word directly to them. Furthermore, they refuse to cite their prophetic sources.

The problem here is, what if the prophetic word is erroneous. Then the off word is going to spread like a wildfire in prophetic circles as it is rereleased over and over again without anyone thinking to judge it. Citing our prophetic sources also gives the hearers the ability to have an opportunity to judge for themselves. Maybe a listener knows something about the track record of the originator of the prophecy that would give them caution about running with the word without more careful consideration. For the sake of the health and accountability of the prophetic church, I believe prophets should cite their prophetic sources,especially in matters of politics, government, and current events.

Although the prophetic movement has been monumental, we have also seen the entrance of charlatans, witches, warlocks, and those who simply haven't been called take major stages and platforms among us. This means that unqualified people are releasing words over people which means we have the prophetic responsibility to cite our sources and at the least judge words before we share them with others. Also, knowing someone's track record alone may not be enough. Someone can be accurate today and veer off tomorrow. By keeping healthy Bible based habits, we can proactively protect the people of God and the authenticity of the prophetic movement from buckling under the demonic pressures that seek to assert influence over the people of God. Without judging prophecy, the prophetic movement will create prophetic cults that are more attuned to their desires or opinions than the Spirit of God.

TRYING TIMES

Many of the prophetic voices releasing words on COVID-19 have little understanding of what the virus is or what the pandemic means for the people that we serve. Leaders have ignorantly downplayed the season the Earth is facing. Some due to ignorance, but others due to an unhealthy political bias.

As I write this book in May 2020, there have been millions of cases of a novel strain of coronavirus that was first discovered in Wuhan, China in December 2019. This new strain of coronavirus abbreviated COVID-19 has overwhelmed hospital systems worldwide and has killed hundreds of thousands of people.

The virus has disrupted our way of life in every way possible from social distancing measures to severe economic disruption. Even with extreme measures in place, cases continue to mount and bodies continue to pile up. If you're a leader with a compassionate heart, even if you don't know anyone with the virus, you perceive the heart of the Father longing to console and comfort a world under immense trauma.

While millions across the world are deluged in grief, anxiety, anguish, and trauma, many have played the role of contrarians aiming to downplay the COVID-19 by comparing it to the flu. Understand that COVID-19 is no flu. Before making claims that run contrary to medical experts, we ought to first understand the basics behind what we're dealing with. Furthermore, if we're going to prophecy about it, we should understand what we're prophesying about.

Stages of COVID-19

1. Dry Cough, Fever, Headache
2. Shortness of breath, hypoxia
3. SIRS/Shock, Cardiac Failure, ARDS

Adapted from: COVID-19 Illness in Native and Immunosuppressed States: A Clinical-Therapeutic Staging Proposal Journal of Heart and Lung Transplantation by Hasan K. Siddiqi, MD, MSCR and Mandeep R. Mehra

COVID-19 is a coronavirus that moves in three stages. Some may avoid having the symptoms listed in the figure above because the virus has been found to be asymptomatic. In other words, someone can have the virus without showing any symptoms while passing the pathogens onto other people without knowing it.[11] In the first stage, the virus causes symptoms that are no different than what some might consider a cold. As the virus progresses, the disease becomes more problematic.

In the second stage, patients contract a viral pneumonia as the infection multiplies in the lungs. In stage two, patients often require hospitalization for "observation and management." Some patients even develop hypoxia, where the body isn't receiving enough oxygen, hence the need for ventilators.

A small percentage of patients arrive at stage three where they develop severe inflammatory response syndrome. In stage three, patients may undergo problems like shock, respiratory failure, or cardiac failure.

In summary, COVID-19 is not the flu, but a significant three stage respiratory disease that can cause considerable harm or death. While the majority of the people who contract the disease will recover, the disease has the potential to continue to kill thousands of people because there is currently no vaccine or licensed treatment to effectively combat it. In the current range of scientific understanding of the disease, those with pre-existing conditions, particularly those who are immunocompromised, seem to be the most vulnerable.

Many brush off this fact by saying that the probability for contraction of the disease for most people is quite low or less than one percent. While there may be some truth to that, this is what we call in mathematics and engineering a naive approach to understanding probability. Someone's probability of contracting the disease is based on several factors that scientists are still investigating. Furthermore, in the American context, millions of people are immunocompromised.[12] Thus, in a fairly speculative sense, several millions of Americans are likely to be more susceptible to the disease.

Some go as far as to say, "People die, what's the big deal? This is no different than the flu." That naive and compassionless comparison doesn't add up. In recent years, flu deaths have ranged from 12,000-56,000.[13] The tens of thousands of yearly deaths came over the span of the entire flu season, while the novel coronavirus caused 100,000 deaths in just four months.[14] Even with extreme economy crippling mitigation measures like social distancing and stay-at-home orders, 100,000 people still died in just four months. There's no telling how many would have died if policy-makers didn't prescribe such intense mitigation measures.

Furthermore, frontline observation of COVID-19 shows that the disease is killing far more people than the flu. According to medical practitioners, "The demand on hospital resources during the COVID-19 crisis has not occurred before in the US, even during the worst of influenza seasons. Yet, public officials continue to draw comparisons between seasonal influenza and SARS-CoV-2 [COVID-19] mortality, often in an attempt to minimize the effects of the unfolding pandemic."[15]

Prophetic people who are comparing COVID-19 to the flu and downplaying the strength of the virus are out of touch with the reality of what's happening on the ground. Knowing the numbers and being aware of the statistics doesn't mean that we are living in fear. We can't defeat any enemy that we're uninformed about.

Regardless of the numbers, I believe that it's time to have a real conversation about how indifferent American Christinaity has become. We have become so compassionless that many of us don't care about the sudden death of thousands of mothers, fathers, husbands, wives, brothers, and sisters all across the country. We've become so content with our knowledge and revelation of the Bible that we've become unaffected by the pain of people.

The insensitivity of the believer to the brokenness

and grief of a hurting world is why church attendance is down and we don't see many miracles. If the body of Christ in America is at the point where we can say, "who cares, people die" in the middle of a pandemic, we've become not much more than a collective of blind Pharisees leading other blind Pharisees. Such blindness means that we are preaching a powerful holy gospel that has no effect because of our arrogant and graceless approach to people.

You might say that such a rebuke is harsh and unwarranted. You might still not see the big deal until COVID-19 hits in a sensitive spot like your home or family. It's easy to lack compassion when you're unaffected, but when you or someone that you love has lungs that are under the elephant like pressure of COVID-19, compassion won't be too far from you.

The problem is that if we're going to live as the scripture teaches, then we must learn to have compassion even when we're untouched. The power of God's grace manifests when we submit ourselves to the Spirit of God in such a way that the pain of another becomes our pain.

Jesus wants us to care deeply about the grief that our nation is in and He wants us to be concerned for every soul. A Christianity that is distant from the pain and brokenness of the human condition is one that will have limited reach and impact in the world. Furthermore, when we are so callous to the trouble around us, we open ourselves up to being prime candidates for the judgement of the Almighty. God rebuked Israel for their hardened hearts toward the pain of their brethren through the prophet Amos.

*4"Woe to those who lie on beds of ivory
and stretch themselves out on their couches,
and eat lambs from the flock
and calves from the midst of the stall,
5 who sing idle songs to the sound of the harp
and like David invent for themselves
instruments of music,
6 who drink wine in bowls
and anoint themselves with the finest oils,
but are not grieved over the ruin of Joseph!
7 Therefore they shall now be the first
of those who go into exile,
and the revelry of those who stretch
themselves out shall pass away."
-Amos 6:4-7*

God prophesied judgement on people who were not grieved by the circumstances of another. They were not grieved by the judgement of their nearby community so God declared judgement on those who were at ease.

The overwhelming number of deaths should bring

the people of God to repentance, weeping, and prayer. How can we solve problems that we're unmoved by? When we look at the life and ministry of Jesus Christ, not only did He shed blood, but He also bled compassion. It was the focal point of His miracle ministry.

> *"And Jesus went throughout all the cities and villages, teaching in their synagogues and proclaiming the gospel of the kingdom and healing every disease and every affliction. When He saw the crowds, He had compassion for them, because they were harassed and helpless, like sheep without a shepherd."*
> *-Matthew 10:36-37*

Jesus didn't look at the crowds and say, "I'm healthy, what's their problem? Why can't they just pray like me and get where I'm at?" He didn't look at broken people and use them as a measuring stick to coat his ego as we often do.

Our self-righteousness and our pride is filling the space where our compassion should be. We want people to pull themselves up by the bootstraps instead of crying out and receiving intervention from God almighty. For this reason, we don't see the miracle ministry of Jesus flowing effortlessly as it should.

We're in a time where many pastors and leaders are demanding state governments to permit them to open their services. Lawsuits have been filed and some pastors have even died from COVID-19 in defiance. There are church members across the nation who want to go back to church as usual.

It seems that we want the doors of the church to open so that we can have our church and our tradition. Many want the church to be open simply so they can come back to a place of normalcy and have their peace. Others want the church to be open because they believe it's their constitutional right. They're fighting for principle and value, but there's something missing from the conversation.

I believe that every ministry leader in America should be weeping. As we hear the numbers on the news and read the scientific papers, there should be a wail for the loss. As we hear of countless preachers and leaders who have died and the many churches that have closed permanently, there should be a groan that comes out.

Maybe I missed it, but I haven't heard many advocates for ending church quarantine say that they want to gather together to cry, moan, and wail. We want to have church, but my question is where is the cry? Some, just a few that I've seen, have talked about opening churches for prayer. I believe that we are in an unusual time. The remedy is not in fighting for what seems to be our constitutional right to assemble, but rather in crying out before the Lord.

If we view everything as a conspiracy, when will we

ever allow ourselves to feel the pain of the season to cry out before the Lord? When did you have your last weep? Even if the crisis we are in were to be the matter of some deep state conspiracy, should not our hearts break for the demented souls of those involved in such things? Shouldn't we then bombard heaven with intercession for them? Shouldn't we be broken for the thousands of lives lost?

America needs to wake up and come out of slumber. Come out of the comfort of knowing that you and yours are doing fine and then weep. Come out of the comfort of thinking that you know so much about the world around you and weep.

This is a time of Joel 2:17 where we should be looking not simply to assemble the flock, but the ministers and the elders should be looking for a place to weep.

> *"Between the vestibule and the altar*
> *let the priests, the ministers of the Lord, weep*
> *and say, 'Spare your people, O Lord,*
> *and make not your heritage a reproach,*
> *a byword among the nations.*
> *Why should they say among the peoples,*
> *'Where is their God?'"*
> *-Joel 2:27*

GLOBAL GOSSIP

Conspiracy theories are all about challenging the established explanation or understanding of something and suggesting some covert group is at the center of it. They point the finger at individuals and organizations without any verifiable information.

Ultimately these theories are no more than gossip aimed at the governmental level. As Christians, we should have the mind of Christ and not engage in gossip that feeds our carnal nature.

"The words of a whisperer are like delicious morsels;
they go down into the inner parts of the body."
- Proverbs 18:9

When we gossip, we are projecting our ideas, imaginations, judgments, and criticisms of people without the proper knowledge base to view them objectively. In order for gossip to spread, it doesn't have to be rooted in truth, it simply needs to be attractive to the flesh.

We get disappointed when others slander our name and misrepresent our character, but somehow we find joy in spreading rumors about politicians, scientists, and world leaders that we've never met.

Every time we pick up the mouse to post, share, and comment on conspiratorial rumors, we align ourselves with the enemy's objective to falsely demean a life or organization. Every time we use the internet to accuse someone of murder, global plots, or other conspiracy theories, we are doing the enemy's job for him concerning that individual. We're spreading hatred, accusations, and word curses on someone's husband or wife, mother or father, son or daughter.

That someone has hopes, dreams, fears, insecurities, and emotions just like you do. I pray that some of us never become famous or significant figures in the public eye because I fear that we will reap the anger and distrust that we sowed.

Of course, we should not be naive, nor should we lack prudence and blindly trust anything that a leader or an expert says. Rather, my argument is that we should not be sources or promoters of garbage information because it causes people to make dangerous decisions. Anyone can post information online regardless of the source.

Gossipping about your best friend may not have life or death consequences. However, as we've already explored, Alex Jones's gossip led to the torment and harassment of Sandy Hook parents. Even if you don't have a platform as large as InfoWars, you do have a social circle.

Let's say scientists develop a verifiably safe cure for COVID-19 and it has absolutely nothing to do with the mark of the beast in the book of Revelation. Let's also say that you share a post from a random website that says the COVID-19 cure is a poison. Consequently, someone dies from COVID-19 because they are too afraid to receive the cure. Unfortunately, the blood is on your hands. If scientists develop a vaccine and you share a post about how Bill Gates created the vaccine to in-act marshall law, then you better make sure you're right. Because if just one person that follows you doesn't take the vaccine and starts an outbreak, then the blood is on your hands.

Don't let others die because of your paranoia or gossip. If you're going to spread conspiracy theories and breed mistrust, understand the weight and consequence of what you post. Understand that you need to make sure that you've done the fact checking and critically examined what you're encouraging people to believe because what you share could cost some their lives. Not only should we be accurate when we prophecy, we should aim to be accurate with what we report to others as fact.

So many COVID-19 theories are simply erroneous, yet and still many prophetic people have used these bogus sources of hearsay to fuel prophecy or confirm what they believe God to be saying. If the Lord does show someone a conspiracy, they should never align with a source of gossip or misinformation as confirmation of what they saw or heard. If it is the Word of the Lord, it will come to pass in time. There's no need to hastily partner with a spirit of gossip, confusion, and delusion to confirm a prophetic word. The spirit of God has a different agenda that stands diametrically opposed to the spirit of suspicion and gossip that fuels so many conspiracy theories. God wants his people to live in the truth. The enemy wants his people to be gullible, skeptical, and lawless.

Exposure from God leads to repentance, conviction, and change. The conviction of the spirit would lead us to cry out for conspirators and enemies in deep intercession and prayer. We would get off of Facebook and get on our faces before God to cry for the deliverance of their souls rather than deem them as evil and unredeemable.

Can the average believer who has aligned themselves with conspiratorial thinking stand before Bill Gates, Dr. Fauchi or any other figure whom they accuse as being masterminds behind COVID-19 and minister to them out of love. Is the average prophet who holds the views of sites like InfoWars disciplined enough to press beyond their biases and say what God is currently saying to them and not begin to prophecy their own judgements from their soul? Sadly, I don't believe that most can separate their suspicion from the unction of the Holy Ghost when those they perceive to be as the heralds of the New World Order arrive. If the blood of Jesus is powerful enough to save you, why is it not strong enough to deliver those that you dislike, disagree with and frankly hate? Have we become so spiritually astute that we believe that our election to the divine grace of God was earned in a way that even a satan worshipper couldn't earn? The same blood required to save us can be used to redeem anyone the Father sees fit. Let's not allow the lens of suspicion to become a source for judgement. Our biases should not hinder deliverance.

DEBUNKING POPULAR THEORIES

How Prophets Should Handle Genuine Conspiratorial Words from the Lord

If the Lord does give you a Word regarding a conspiracy or a plot regarding people in high places, do not rely on conspiracy theory websites or other fake news outlets as a source of confirmation or validation for what God is saying to you. Trust God, wait on the Lord and his word will come to pass in due time. Many prophets in the Old Testament did not live to see what they prophesied. Our job is to declare what God is saying not rely on sources of misinformation to be confirmation. When we do so, the governmental powers that may need to rely on our ability to hear God in the future will be skeptical at lending their ears to prophetic voices that can't differentiate fact from fiction. Much of what's on the internet regarding COVID-19 is pure fiction. Just because we find information on Google doesn't mean that the information is indeed valid. Anyone can post anything on the internet. Prophets need to verify the information they're posting especially if they're from an alternative source. Do understand that you can't validate a biased alternative news source with another biased alternative news source. That's just like verifying the authenticity of gossip you heard from another gossiper. Peer reviewed academic research and journalistic institutions that are required by law to uphold certain standards should be regarded with more credibility than blogs and youtube videos that anyone can spew governmental gossip on. If there are no journalistic or ethical standards that your news sources have to abide by you should not trust them. Speak the Word of God and it will be confirmed when it comes to pass. Below are some popular conspiracy theories riddled with junk science and pure misinformation so that people can capitalize off of the fear of the hour rather than God's clarity.

COVID-19 Is Caused By 5G

This is something that I've seen prophets not only comment on but also "prophecy." Let's be honest. Many of the people advancing claims that 5G is causing the novel coronavirus have no clue what 5G even stands for let alone how the technology works.

The theory began in Europe[16] and spread even faster than the pandemic. Conspiracy theorists have been taking advantage of the global crisis to make money. Some are even selling USB flash drives that are supposed to protect people from the supposed harmful 5G waves. This conspiracy theory continued to gain much traction as a video of what was claimed to be Chinese citizens tearing down 5G towers to destroy the virus. In actuality, the footage originated from the 2019 Hong Kong protests where the citizens were not tearing down a 5G tower, but a smart lamppost.[17]

I believe Dr. Ham from Mount Elizabeth Novena Hospital, summarized things best, "The virus is extremely sneaky and has exceeded all expectations of other viral infections, but they have not learned the skill of teleportation via the electric cables — and certainly not true electromagnetic waves via the 5G."[18]

Taking a trip back to high school biology or chemistry class easily debunks the theory. A virus is a parasite that lacks the capacity to reproduce on its own. Once attached to a host it can efficiently hack cells to aid in reproduction.Viruses, which are made of organic material, molecules, DNA, RNA, etc., cannot hop into the digital world. Since the source of their survival and replication is with living creatures, what would their evolutionary incentive to do so even be?

Furthermore, 5G is the fifth generation wireless network technology standard that, like other wireless technologies, uses radio waves. These radio-waves emit non-ionizing radiation. The concern for 5G or any other radio wave technology would not be viruses teleporting, but rather cancer. Much of the academic literature has found no connection between non-ionizing radiation and cancer, or even other human health impacts for that matter. However, most of this research hails from the 1980s.[19]

Scientists in the past few years have been sounding the alarm, about potential cancer causing effects and sperm damage.[20] Over 200 scientists actually signed the International EMF Scientist Appeal to call on governments to reconsider radiation exposure limits that they believe are too high.[21] In summary, we shouldn't be worried about COVID-19 spreading via 5G, but instead there may be other potential health issues like cancer.

How Can They Predict COVID-19 and It's Second Wave If They Didn't Plan It

Some question how can one predict a pandemic if it's not planned. The answer in a sense is the same way that you can predict what time you're going to bed today, past behavior.

Epidemiologists, data scientists, machine learning researchers use data about past behavior, the spread of infectious diseases and the nature of viruses to calculate how diseases will spread. Prophets around the country sound quite ignorant to political leaders who they should be in the room with when they say things like "how can they see it coming if they didn't plan it?" Bayes rule, probabilistic analysis, temporal fourier analysis in concert with decades of studying the nature and spread of diseases is how health practitioners can predict the spread of infectious diseases. Ignorance is keeping many prophetic voices out of the rooms that they're called to sit in. The second wave of COVID-19 is obvious due to the mathematics of easing of COVID-19 regulations vs. the reproducibility of the virus. Scientists have been using mathematics and plotting charts with predictions because of an empirical understanding that God has blessed the world to have. The church may want to wake up and listen.

Bill Gates Has a Patent to COVID-19

No one has faced more ire from the prophetic community than Bill Gates. There's a 2015 video of Bill Gates giving a TED Talk on the potential of the next global pandemic. Many ignorantly took the video out of context and assumed that because he forewarned of it, he must have created it. That's the equivalent to a prophet foreseeing an earthquake and then people blaming him for causing the event. It's odd how prophetic people are at odds with someone for foreseeing a problem ahead of time. I believe that since God can't get us to listen through the prophets, He has to speak through academics, scientists, and researchers like Bill Gates. Gates did not predict the pandemic on his own knowledge alone. As a prudent voice of counsel for governments in public policy, Gates is well aware of at least three decades of academic research forewarning of the potential for pandemic scale events and the need to prepare. A simple search in Google Scholar will reveal decades of academic papers warning of potential outbreak on the scale of what we're seeing with COVID-19 today. Plainly Gates, was far from the first one to foresee the global problem that we're facing today. Dedicated scientists and government advisors have been predicting this for years and trying to warn governments.

Conspiracy theory websites and prophets alike have been saying that Gates has the patent for COVID-19. This erroneous claim is very misleading. A coronavirus is a form of virus that causes respiratory illness. There are many types of coronaviruses like SARs or even the common cold and bronchitis. COVID-19 is what one would describe as a novel, or not previously detected type of coronavirus. The COVID-19 strand, which comes from SARS-coV-2, has a publicly available genome so that we can research and study it.[22] In other words, there is no patent. You and I can go online and analyze the genome right now for free.

What the alternative media outlets are trying to do

is to stretch the truth by saying
a patent owned by the Pirbright Institution belongs to Bill Gates since they received Gates Foundation funding. The Pirbright Institution is an organization that does research on zoonotic diseases (diseases transferred from animals to humans) like coronaviruses and other respiratory illnesses. In fact the patent that the Pirbright owns is not for COVID-19, but a vaccine for a type of coronavirus.[23] Even the patent and the genetic code is publicly available online.

Therefore the Gates Foundation did not fund an organization with a patent on COVID-19. It funded an organization that does scientific research on zoonotic diseases to help prevent outbreaks like we're seeing today. Just because an institution does research on coronaviruses does not mean that they created COVID-19. We actually need to fund a lot more research on coronaviruses and other zoonotic diseases to be prepared for future pandemic scale outbreaks. If there had been more research funding available for organizations that research coronaviruses, maybe we wouldn't be suffering as much today because we might have a vaccine or at least a treatment.

Hospitals Are Cooking The Books and the Pandemic Is Fake
There has been a lot of discussion among skep-

tics regarding the accounting method for COVID-19 deaths. Some have gone as far to say that hospitals are overcounting coronavirus deaths in order to earn more money. What commentators should take the time to understand is the medical nature of the disease. Doctors report that in most cases, determining the cause of death is very easy as the virus may cause the lungs to be "two to three times or more the normal weight of a normal lung."[24]

In other cases, the determination may be more difficult because COVID-19 triggers or exacerbates health problems from pre-existing conditions. Earlier, I explained how the disease progresses in three stages and its particular impact on those with pre-existing health conditions. If someone who comes into the emergency room with pre-existing cardiac conditions tests positive for COVID-19 and dies suddenly, the doctor has to use their best judgement to ascertain whether the death arose strictly from the cardiac issues or whether COVID-19 played a role in the death.

CDC guidelines ask providers to list an UCOD (underlying cause of death) which is " the disease or injury which initiated the train of morbid events leading directly to death" and "other significant conditions that contributed to the death."[25] Medical professionals like doctors and forensic pathologists are competent enough to use their expertise to determine whether COVID-19 was the UCOD or another significant contributor. Even if the nature of COVID-19 makes identifying the UCOD of certain deaths difficult, a recent study has already shown that COVID-19 deaths have actually been undercounted. An analysis of mortality data from 22 countries suggests that tens of thousands more people have died from COVID-19 than what has been actually reported. The report also concludes that in the two months preceding the release of the report "far more people have died in most of these countries than in previous years."[26]

Coronavirus deniers have gone as far as to launch a #FilmYourHospital campaign on social media where supposed "truth" vigilantes can prove that COVID-19 is a hoax by finding hospitals with empty parking lots and waiting rooms. While these self-proclaimed vigilantes have spent plenty of time reading tweets and conspiracy theory websites, they haven't taken the time to read the official CDC guidelines that gave hospitals significant recommendations. These recommendations caused empty waiting rooms and parking lots to slow the spread of the virus. For example, the CDC recommended that hospitals "cancel elective procedures, use telemedicine when possible, limit points of entry and manage visitors, screen everyone entering the facility for COVID-19 symptoms"' and "Implement source control for everyone entering the facility, regardless of [their] symptoms."[27] In other words, the CDC gave hospitals very detailed guidance on how to limit people from going to hospitals and block visitors from entry. My wife was pregnant at the time of COVID-19.

As soon as the outbreak hit my state, we were screened for symptoms at the door. In fact, towards the end of her last trimester, I was no longer able to come into the office for our baby check-ups because of visitation limits. Thankfully, I was permitted into the labor room for delivery, but no one in our family was allowed to see our newborn while we were in the hospital.

Unfortunately, in New York, many men were not allowed into the delivery room and this caused many women to to have to go through the delivery process by themselves.[28] By reducing services and adjusting key waiting room policies, hospitals lowered the potential for exposure of the virus. Contrary to the beliefs of the conspiracy theorists, the empty hospitals weren't a reason to validate that the coronavirus didn't exist. Intead, an attempt to mitigate an aggressively spreading virus.

While this is not an exhaustive list, most COVID-19 conspiracy theories can be debunked with the proper informational context. Conspiracy theorists when challenged often refuse to respond to scientific critique and accuse any challenger of being a part of the conspiracy. Science ought not be refuted with gossip, but with proper investigation and through research.

WISDOM FOR PASTORS AND LEADERS IN CRISIS

Unless you were a pastor in the early 20th century during the Spanish flu pandemic or even during one of the significant cholera outbreaks, you probably have never been a leader during a regional epidemic, let alone a global pandemic.

Navigating an unseen season can be incredibly difficult. In recent years, no one has pastored during a global pandemic. Thus, we are in a time where few people have the experiential wisdom to act as guides.

Being a leader in a time like this can feel lonely and isolating. Those in hotspot cities can be under immense mourning and emotional fatigue. Any compassionate leader is going to be concerned with the illnesses and deaths of members in their congregation.

As if pastoral matters weren't enough, leaders are also faced with the reality of how the virus affects their city .Seeing the halt of church services, lay-offs, and the stress on hospital systems can bring any leader additional grief. Many of us also have to deal with the loss of ministry colleagues, all while also ministering to those who we serve who have suffered a loss, too.

With such a difficult climate and context, every leader needs to make self-care a priority. The enemy would love to make God's chief generals burnout in the midst of a crisis and fall into his hand for insanity and backslide.

The HALT acronym stands for hungry, angry, lonely, and tired. It has been said that we are most likely to sin or have a significant fall when we are in one of those states. In this season, the truth is that we may even be feeling all four of these states and emotions at one time.

If we take care of the flock without taking care of ourselves, we will succumb to the weaknesses of our humanity. We should not depend on our own strength as superhumans, but rather on the strength of God. We must recognize our limitations, our weak points, and ask God for help.

I know that many of us are working tirelessly in the areas of preaching,, community engagement, social justice, and social entrepreneurship. coHowever, this does not negate the fact that we must take the necessary time to rest.

Leaders do not have time to lose time by being so busy that they have no space to rest. In addition to getting the proper sleep, leaders also need spiritual rest which only comes from spending quality time with Jesus. This is not the hour to reduce or skip out on prayer and Bible reading. We need more of God than ever. Private intimate time with Him is the only way that we can have the strength that we need to navigate the complexities of this crisis. If we don't rest, we won't be able to run with the visions and ideas that God has filled us with.

This is also a great time and space to rethink the way that we've been approaching church. Quarantine can be a blessing if we allow it to be. In the past decade, there are so many leaders who have not even taken one sabbatical from their ministry assignments.

In rest, revelation comes. If we never rest and reflect, we will not evaluate our efforts, activities, and the motives that drive them. By taking time away from the traditional Sunday service, leaders can consider areas that have been very fruitful for their ministries. They can also reflect upon the areas that have been ineffective and unfruitful.

This opportunity to step back and see things for the way they really are can be a great benefit. It is difficult to objectively evaluate the growth, progress, and effectiveness of something while you are intimately involved with it.

Due to the pandemic, there's been an increase in virtual church attendance and I believe leaders should be proactive about how to handle that change. Instead of being content with the temporary increase of members, churches should be thinking ahead. These numbers can immediately decrease once quarantine is over. Therefore, every leader should be spending time evaluating how to effectively proceed with training and discipling their new potential digital partners that were not visiting before.

Despite the quarantine restrictions, the digital world has made it such that many churches are actually in a place of growth, momentum, and transition. Momentum must be managed. We should not be content with momentum, but rather proper stewards of it before it comes to a regretful crash.

Concerning our approach to in-person ministry, several things need to change if we are to stand in the days to come. Many are prophesying revival and I too believe this to be the word of the Lord. However, every word must be managed. We play an important role in keeping who God sends us once the revival is over.

If we approach church the same way we did before the pandemic began, we're simply going to expose a larger audience to our dysfunctional and inconsistent habits that don't measure up to the Word of God. We've got a lot of changes to make in a short amount of time. In my estimation, the most crucial change we need to make is our approach to discipleship.

Jesus didn't say we need to make believers. He said we need to make disciples. He didn't say make people who say a 20 second salvation prayer. He said make disciples. I believe that we've created an event based Christianity. Instead of focusing on the biblical model of discipleship, or the ministry of multiplication, Sunday has become the main show. In the Bible, disciples make disciples who are mature and fully formed in the Word of God. The pressure on the pulpit then is to create not to simply preach. Rather the focus should be to build a culture of discipleship where even the senior leaders are actively engaged in discipleship beyond the four walls of the church. The pressure on the pews then is for them to be more than casual hearers excited to hear a brilliant orator, but rather be disciples that make other disciples.

This cannot be done with our biblically illiterate approach to catechizing new believers. As the cancer of misinformation continues to spread throughout the world, the church is going to have to get far better at biblical training. Much of the American church is biblically illiterate and has no understanding of the fundamental doctrines of the Christian faith.

The revival of ancient religions and a growing desire to be spiritually "woke" should be sending ministry leaders to their Bibles to study more. Just like there are conspiracy theories regarding COVID-19, there are an innumerable amount of conspiracy theories circulating regarding Christianity and the origins of the Bible.

If we did a better job of training new believers in theology, apologetics, soteriology, pneumatology, and church history, we would not be so weak to the demonic movements snatching our youth from faith in Christ. Leaders should be using this time to figure out how to combat opposition from the various sects aiming to pervert the ears of God's sheep.
It's of no surprise to me that youth go to college and never return to the faith. Since we did not disciple them, what more can we expect?

As we were getting our praise and breakthrough, they were playing videogames on their phones or texting. We rebuked them about not paying attention in school, but let them do anything they wanted on their phones at church because we were unconcerned with discipling them. If God is sending us a harvest, we must fix our broken training and discipleship methods.

This is very important in the prophetic movement because we are very spiritual, profoundly supernatural, but very poor in biblical training. The average prophet can't even give a summary of the texts of the Old Testament prophets, let alone explain the difference between Calvinism and Arminianism. Everyone has an end-times word, but few can express the difference between premillennialism and postmillennialism when asked.

Do our prophetic people know who Tyndale, Wesley, or Calvin are? Furthermore, do they really understand the work of Bishop Charles Harrison Mason? How can we prophecy and truly discern the future unless we have a true foundation of the history that brought us here?

That's one reason why so much false prophecy persists. People don't understand the fundamentals and the parameters that the scriptures give us. What God says today will never contradict what He said yesterday.

As one of my brothers, Prophet Angelow Hickson, often says, "It's time to sit the body of Christ down in a classroom." If we don't fix our training culture, we are going to lose the harvest to come.

Now is the time to arise and not do church as usual. Once we return, it's not time to have church like the good ole times. It's time to have church the way God intended. It's time for us to break the barriers that have been holding back the supernatural move of God. It's time for us to see the church that God intended from the beginning. It's time for leaders in the midst of this pandemic to re-think the 21st century church.

A CLOSING
PROPHETIC WORD

I've spoken a lot about what I don't believe God said. In closing, I leave you with what the Lord has shared with me about COVID-19. Although things are difficult now, we will recover. By the grace of God, there will be great recovery and new voices will emerge from the ashes. New prophetic voices will emerge that will shake the Earth. The Lord said to me that there are prophets who He's had in hiding for so long that don't have an ego, nor do they want to be seen. They're going to bring direction, comfort, and clarity to the nations of the Earth. They will guide and direct the developing nations that are open to the prophetic.

The Father also said to me that this is an hour to invest wisely. Despite economic confusion in the days to come, we will indeed see economic recovery. The people of God should make investments in the market so that they will reap the rewards later.

Additionally, God gave me a stern warning for the

governments of the world. COVID-19 is just the beginning for the troubles that are to come. Although we will recover from this crisis, there are many more to come due to the rising global temperatures. Events like COVID-19 will take effect in every aspect of society. We will see the arrival of new diseases and a revival of outbreaks of old diseases like cholera. Diseases like dengue fever and West Nile virus will spread to new locations in the decades to come. There will be significant reproductive and fertility issues among women due to the spread of infectious agents.

The United States in particular must rapidly fix her aging infrastructure or there will come a day when the land regrets the negligence. America also needs to address its hospital capacity issues because COVID-19 will not be the last outbreak of epidemic scale to touch the homeland. Destruction is coming, but there are many things that can be prevented if leaders stop procrastinating. This is an hour of humbling that the deaf ears of leaders across the globe can repent and prepare for the difficulties to come.

COVID-19 is simply a precursor of what is to come. The Lord said that if governments don't take time to hear Him, they will see the demise of many in the coming days. God has answers, strategies, and solutions, but our government leaders must have an ear to hear how to prepare for what is to come. In particular, the turn of the century will be a very difficult time for the Earth. However, the Lord is sending His prophets with answers like rain. The question is this: will the nations of the Earth listen to the answers that God sends in the days to come?

REFERENCES

1. Says:, K., Says:, P., & Says:, T. (2019, June 26). Higher Intelligence And An Analytical Thinking Style Offer No Protection Against "The Illusory Truth Effect" – Our Tendency To Believe Repeated Claims Are True. Retrieved from https://digest.bps.org.uk/2019/06/26/higher-intelligence-and-an-analytical-thinking-style-offer-no-protection-against-the-illusory-truth-effect-our-tendency-to-believe-repeated-claims-are-more-likely-to-be-true/

2. Hasher, L., Goldstein, D., & Toppino, T. (1977). Frequency and the conference of referential validity. *Journal of Verbal Learning and Verbal Behavior, 16*(1), 107-112. doi:10.1016/s0022-5371(77)80012-1

3. Fazio, L. K., & Marsh, E. J. (2009). Prior knowledge does not protect against illusory truth effects. *PsycEXTRA Dataset*. doi:10.1037/e520562012-049

4. FBI Says No One Killed at Sandy Hook. (2014, September 25). Retrieved from https://www.infowars.com/fbi-says-no-one-killed-at-sandy-hook/

5. Baddour, D., & Selby, W. G. (2016, September 1). PolitiFact - Hillary Clinton correct that Austin's Alex Jones said no one died at Sandy Hook Elementary. Retrieved from https://www.politifact.com/factchecks/2016/sep/01/hillary-clinton/hillary-clinton-correct-austins-alex-jones-said-no/

6. Lindsay, R. (2019, March 29). Alex Jones Lists His Sources for Sandy Hook Conspiracy Theories. Retrieved from https://www.ny-times.com/video/us/100000006435844/alex-jones-deposition-sandy-hook.html

7. https://www.youtube.com/watch?v=FuqjmP959vo

8. H. (Producer). (2019, March 29). *Alex Jones' Deposition On Sandy Hook Shooting* [Video file]. Retrieved 2020, from https://www.youtube.com/watch?v=FuqjmP959vo

9. Chappell, B. (2020, May 11). Wuhan Reports New COVID-19 Cases - The City's 1st In More Than A Month. Retrieved from https://www.npr.org/sections/coronavirus-live-updates/2020/05/11/853731869/wuhan-reports-new-covid-19-cases-the-first-in-more-than-a-month

10. Siddiqi, H. K., & Mehra, M. R. (2020). COVID-19 illness in native and immunosuppressed states: A clinical–therapeutic staging proposal. *The Journal of Heart and Lung Transplantation, 39*(5), 405-407. doi:10.1016/j.healun.2020.03.012

11. Mizumoto, K., Kagaya, K., Zarebski, A., & Chowell, G. (2020, March 12). Estimating the asymptomatic proportion of coronavirus disease 2019 (COVID-19) cases on board the Diamond Princess cruise ship, Yokohama, Japan, 2020. Retrieved 2020, from https://www.eurosurveillance.org/content/10.2807/1560-7917.ES.2020.25.10.2000180/

12. Shall, T. (n.d.). How Many Americans are Immuno-compromised? " Berman Institute Bioethics Bulletin. Retrieved 2020, from http://bioethicsbulletin.org/archive/how-many-americans-are-immunocompromised

13. How Is Pandemic Flu Different from Seasonal Flu?

(2019, May 07). Retrieved from https://www.cdc.gov/flu/pandemic-resources/basics/about.html

14. Villarreal, A. (2020, May 28). Four months and 100,000 deaths: The defining Covid-19 moments in the US – timeline. Retrieved 2020, from https://www.theguardian.com/us-news/2020/apr/25/us-coronavirus-timeline-trump-cases-deaths

15. Faust, J. S., & Rio, C. D. (2020). Assessment of Deaths From COVID-19 and From Seasonal Influenza. *JAMA Internal Medicine*. doi:10.1001/jamainternmed.2020.2306

16. Ahmed, W., Vidal-Alaball, J., Downing, J., & Seguí, F. L. (2020). COVID-19 and the 5G Conspiracy Theory: Social Network Analysis of Twitter Data. *Journal of Medical Internet Research, 22*(5). doi:10.2196/19458

17. Video does not show 5G pole being torn down in China. (2020, April 03). Retrieved from https://apnews.com/afs:Content:8723301797

18. Cher, A. (2020, May 01). Don't hold your breath. Experts debunk dangerous myths about the coronavirus. Retrieved from https://www.cnbc.com/2020/05/01/experts-explain-why-coronavirus-myths-misinformation-can-be-dangerous.html

19. Moskowitz, J. (2019, October 17). We Have No Reason to Believe 5G Is Safe. Retrieved 2020, from https://blogs.scientificamerican.com/observations/we-have-no-reason-to-believe-5g-is-safe/

20. Miller, A. B., Sears, M. E., Morgan, L. L., Davis, D. L., Hardell, L., Oremus, M., & Soskolne, C. L. (2019). Risks to Health and Well-Being From Radio-Frequency Radiation Emitted by Cell Phones and Other Wireless Devices. *Frontiers in Public Health, 7*. doi:10.3389/fpubh.2019.00223

21. Moskowitz, J. (2019, October 17). We Have

No Reason to Believe 5G Is Safe. Retrieved 2020, from https://blogs.scientificamerican.com/observations/we-have-no-reason-to-believe-5g-is-safe/

22. SARS-CoV-2 (Severe acute respiratory syndrome coronavirus 2) Sequences. (n.d.). Retrieved from https://www.ncbi.nlm.nih.gov/genbank/sars-cov-2-seqs/

23. T. (2015). U.S. Patent No. EP 3 172 319 B1. Washington, DC: U.S. Patent and Trademark Office.

24. Pappas, S. (2020, May 19). How COVID-19 Deaths Are Counted. Retrieved from https://www.scientificamerican.com/article/how-covid-19-deaths-are-counted1/

25. COVID-19 Coding and Reporting Guidance - National Vital Statistics System. (2020, May 20). Retrieved from https://www.cdc.gov/nchs/covid19/coding-and-reporting.htm

26. Wu, J., McCann, A., Katz, J., & Peltier, E. (n.d.). 120,000 Missing Deaths: Tracking the True Toll of the Coronavirus Outbreak. *The New York Times*. Retrieved from https://www.nytimes.com/interactive/2020/04/21/world/coronavirus-missing-deaths.html

27. Infection Control Guidance for Healthcare Professionals about Coronavirus (COVID-19). (2020, June 03). Retrieved from https://www.cdc.gov/coronavirus/2019-nCoV/hcp/infection-control.html

28. Wabc. (2020, March 24). Coronavirus Updates: New rules deny birth partners at some NYC hospitals during COVID-19 crisis. Retrieved from https://abc7chicago.com/family/new-rules-deny-birth-partners-at-some-nyc-hospitals-during-covid-19-crisis/6044017/

www.ingramcontent.com/pod-product-compliance
Lightning Source LLC
Chambersburg PA
CBHW060038050426
42448CB00012B/3059